W9-CEO-919

"This work is about "the paradox of crossing, being nowhere yet here," where travelers, family members, and lovers seem perpetually in a state of "almost touching," of "learn[ing] to adore [their] losses." Heartfelt and elegant, these exquisitely crafted poems place Blanco in that pantheon of *poetas* from the Americas who have flourished in the Old World and the New.

Directions to the Beach of the Dead—spanning three continents—marks Richard Blanco as arguably the most cosmopolitan poet of his generation." —Francisco Aragón

"In *Directions to the Beach of the Dead*, Richard Blanco enacts the exile's great conflict in his astonishing, unerring poems of distance and desire, refuge and release. At once pensive and restless, full of both abandonment and abandon, this book is ultimately a journey to the haunted, utterly familiar places in our own hearts. Lost Cuba, newfound love, immemorial time—this soulful poet gives us all that is at once impossible to have ever owned, and yet ever within the reach of our having known." —Rafael Campo

"The universe of Richard Blanco is a place of lush, exhilarating landscapes and kindred souls. Its sweep is both magnificent and intimate in detail. And it shines most gloriously in his latest offering, *Directions to the Beach of the Dead*. His words are honey from Ochún herself." —Liz Balmaseda

"Richard Blanco has written a strong and beautiful book that takes his fine poetry forward to a new and exciting level. While these poems possess a keen sense of past and place, they move beyond nostalgia to the rich difficulties of the nowhere but here that is his clear milieu." —Elizabeth Alexander

"Richard Blanco is a troubadour of Exile . . . with aching stories of its displacement, loss and nostalgia—that uniquely Cuban reverie—for what might have been." —Ann Louise Bardach

DIRECTIONS TO THE BEACH OF THE DEAD

CAMINO DEL SOL

A Latina and Latino Literary Series

DIRECTIONS
TO THE BEACH
OF THE DEAD

Richard Blanco

The University of Arizona Press   Tucson

The University of Arizona Press
© 2005 Richard Blanco
All rights reserved

www.uapress.arizona.edu

Library of Congress Cataloging-in-Publication Data
Blanco, Richard, 1968–
Directions to the beach of the dead / Richard Blanco.
p. cm. — (Camino del sol)
Includes bibliographical references and index.
ISBN 978-0-8165-2479-2 (pbk. : acid-free paper)
1. Cuban Americans—Poetry. 2. Gay men—Poetry.
I. Title. II. Series.
PS3552.L36533D57   2005
811'.54—DC22   2005002649

Publication of this book is made possible in part by
the proceeds of a permanent endowment created with
the assistance of a Challenge Grant from the National
Endowment for the Humanities, a federal agency.

Manufactured in the United States of America on acid-free,
archival-quality paper containing a minimum of 30% post-
consumer waste and processed chlorine free.

17   16   15   14   13   7   6   5   4   3   2

For Sonia, Darden, Carlos, Nikki, Alberto, and Mark.

—*conmigo* everywhere

CONTENTS

~

For when the traveler returns from the mountain-slopes into the valley,

he brings, not a handful of earth, unsayable to others, but instead

some word he has gained, some pure word. . .

RAINER MARIA RILKE, *Duino Elegies*

Time as Art in The Eternal City

The first shadows appear like cells slowly dividing
from every tree and lamppost, while my first words
divide from me onto my journal, trying to capture
how dawn light melts over the city's blank windows,
and its ancient doors, opened a thousand-thousand
mornings to the sun with questions, and closed
on the moon's face without answers. All the days
that have fallen through these courtyards and alleys,
the lives that have worn these cobble stones gray,
all the gray doves that have been cast into flight
by how many church bells? After all the centuries
that have been tolled, hour by hour, and disappeared
above these domes, can it matter that I'm here now:
watching the bougainvillea blaze over the terraces,
counting on the morning to dive into the fountains,
flicker over coins, light the water up with my wishes?
Today, a temple will lose yet another stone that will
continue being a stone, and the Colosseum will move
again through its own shadow. Today, the murdered
and murderers will be remembered and forgotten,
and an empire pardoned for the sake of its beauty
in this city where time is an art. Today, a tourist
once again sits at a café with an espresso, a pen,
waiting to enter the Pantheon, waiting to gaze up
into its oculus, opening like a moonful of sunlight
in its dome, ready to stand in that beam of light,
feel something radiant, and write it down.

A Poet in Venice

Memory's images, once they are fixed in words, are erased, Polo said.
Perhaps I am afraid of losing Venice all at once, if I speak of it.
ITALO CALVINO, *Invisible Cities*

Unlike others, he arrives feeling the train whistling
through him, aware of every step on the platform
and the clatter of trailing his suitcase and his lust
for beauty across the station's rusting shadows
to the laps of water, which he imagines as kisses.

He strolls across foot-bridges, feels the pageantry
of cherubs and marble scrolls under his feet.
Above him, laundry lines turn into rainbows
strung between bare windows laced with violets,
he compares their petals to tears of Murano glass.

On postcards he begins his poems: *Everything
speaks to me here, even the brass eyes of the lions
on the door knockers. In my window, the palazzi
rise like cliffs, enduring the tug of the sea's memory,
the pull of the moon. Today at the Ducale I will…*

At the *Ducale* he imagines himself as a prisoner
crossing the Bridge of Sighs into the dungeons,
carving his name in a wall before dying, believes
this is just as beautiful as the rows of market fruit,
the blood plums he takes pictures of, and devours.

He tastes the Adriatic, craves his warm loneliness
and abandons the map he's carried like a prayer
book, loses himself among the names of saints
until every street ends with his reflection running
into the watercolors of the city over the canals.

Lost in a *campo*, sitting on a granite bench under
the iron swirls of gas lamps and glow of pink glass
blushing the night, he notices the flames flicker
with stray giggles, whispers carried on the wind.
He follows the ricochet of footsteps with his ears,

leading him to the groan of empty gondola hulls,
to the creak of shutters, imagines them closing
like eyelids, and Venice a lover he can't possess
asleep at his side dreaming without him, his eyes
wading alone through the wide-open darkness.

Garden of the Fugitives

We ramble through the column stumps and laugh
when our guide stops at a ruined wall and translates
the irony of its ancient graffiti: *I'm astounded, O wall,*
that you do not crumble under the weight of all these writers.
At the central baths, we all let out a little *oh-wow* when
he explains how they had cold *and* hot running water.
He then leads us through the ruins of the store fronts:
the *Caupona* (or tavern) and the *Pistrinum* (or bakery);
the *Fullonica*, the first laundromat, and the *Thermopolium*,
forerunner to Starbucks, he chuckles. *You could even*
rent a chariot here, he adds, Pompeians were quite advanced.
So they ate, they drank, they bathed, did their laundry—
Gee. We were all getting a little bored, when a man
from Brooklyn finally asked what we all wanted to ask:
Hey, what about the bodies—you know, the casts of those people
gaspin' for life, in the Garden of Fugitives it says right here—
when we gonna see that? Yeah, we all nodded. And we did:
we stared, pointed, took pictures of the dying, and left.

We're Not Going to Malta . . .

because the winds are too strong, our captain announces, his voice like an oracle coming through the loudspeakers in every lounge and hall, as if the ship itself were speaking. We're not going to Malta—*an enchanting island country fifty miles from Sicily,* according to the brochure of the tour we're *not* taking. But what if we did go to Malta? What if, as we are *escorted on foot through the walled "Silent City" of Mdina,* the walls begin speaking to me; and after we *stop a few minutes to admire the impressive architecture,* I feel Malta could be *the* place for me. What if, as we *stroll the bastions to admire the panoramic harbor and stunning countryside,* I dream of buying a little Maltese farm, raising Maltese horses in the green Maltese hills. What if, after we *see the cathedral in Mosta saved by a miracle,* I believe that Malta itself is a miracle; and before I'm *transported back to the pier with a complimentary beverage,* I'm struck with Malta fever, discover I am *very* Maltese indeed, and decide I must return to Malta, learn to speak Maltese with an English (or Spanish) accent, work as a Maltese professor of English at the University of Malta, and teach a course on The Maltese Falcon. Or, what if when we *stop at a factory to shop for famous Malteseware,* I discover that making Maltese crosses is my true passion. Yes, I'd get a Maltese cat *and* a Maltese dog, make Maltese friends, drink Malted milk, join the Knights of Malta, and be happy for the rest of my *Maltesian* life. But we're not going to Malta. Malta is drifting past us, or we are drifting past it—an amorphous hump of green and brown bobbing in the portholes with the horizon as the ship heaves over whitecaps wisping into rainbows for a moment, then dissolving back into the sea.

Through the Straits of Messina, Singing

This could be a basement bar in Boston or an Art Deco lobby in Miami, or a penthouse in Chicago—but it's not. It's the Viking Lounge on the Lido Deck, and we're gliding over Italian waters at twenty-three-hundred hours, straight through the Straits of Messina. We all met yesterday, but right now there's a third drink in everyone's hand, and if you're not drinking, you're smoking; there's a man named Brice with scotch vibrating on his baby grand, and we're Streisand, McLean, or Billy Joel, and all we need to know are the words to *Memories, American Pie,* and *Piano Man,* of course—*man, what are you doing here?* We're singing over our reflections collaged on the piano case, we're sliding between Messina and Sicily's lights, scrolling past us like notes at starboard and port. Between songs, the usual talk: what do you *do's* and where are you *from's*; what we love, what we hate, what we think—even though we'll never see each other again. Then one of us calls out a song and we all say, *Yeah, play that one.* We shut up and sing knowing it all comes down to this: nine strangers on a night like this, when the sea could take us alive, singing, even if we can't remember the lyrics, or keep a tune afloat for more than a minute. Nine strangers knowing almost all the words between them, and just enough about each other for a few seconds of harmony. Nine strangers singing through the two miles between Messina and Sicily, almost touching, almost one, almost closing the sea between them.

In Defense of Livorno

The dove-white hull glides into port just after sunrise. We rise to a hum vibrating from the engine room up to our bunks nine decks above the sea, expecting something postcard-*ish* in the porthole, something very Italian, very Mediterranean. Perhaps an arc of mountains dotted with villas, a legion of sailboat masts at bay, or a harbor of weathered rowboats bobbing on a quilt of seawater greens. Not this sea of blue, yellow, and red freight cars stacked like toy-blocks, not the blotches of oil on the docks, not the acrid grind and burn of diesel engines. At breakfast, from behind tiny glasses of orange juice and porcelain cups of coffee, everyone's eyes are asking: *Where the hell are we?* We're in Livorno, but we're not supposed to see it; we're supposed to herd off the ship into a bus, maneuver through a labyrinth of cargo, ignore the miles of sea wall, and get out of Livorno. We're supposed to pity its empty beaches and bombed-out villas, then cross through the wine and cheese of Tuscany to arrive at Pisa, where we're supposed to follow our guide's orange flag as he marvels over the miscalculation, listen to his reverent whispers lead us through yet another cathedral, to goggle over altars and paintings commissioned with alms. We're supposed to lap-up gelato, buy Tower-of-Pisa ash trays, then skip to Florence where we're supposed to revere the Medici, as we stroll through *their* palazzos, pausing at *their* paintings to say *hmm* and wow and *isn't that amazing.* We're supposed to buy Prada shoes and Gucci belts, get tickets to see David, pretend not to notice his penis, then get back on our bus, awed by the brilliance of humanity, satisfied by beauty all the way back to Livorno. We're not supposed to need Livorno: its barrels of oil and pallets of Chianti, its pounds of prosciutto and cans of coffee, its tons of sugar and made-in-China trinkets. We're not supposed to see anything beautiful here, not even the names glazed over the boxcars—DELMAS, YAN-MING, HAYPAG, MARUBA, CRONOS, MASTO, MARUBA—craned through the sky like new words from the gods, arriving from the very heavens.

Somewhere to Paris

The sole cause of a man's unhappiness
is that he does not know how to stay quietly in his room.
PASCAL, *Pensées*

The *vias* of Italy turn to memory with each turn
and clack of the train's wheels, with every stitch
of track we leave behind, the *duomos* return again
to my imagination, already imagining Paris—
a fantasy of lights and marble that may end
when the train stops at *Gare de l'Est* and I step
into the daylight. In this space between cities,
between the dreamed and the dreaming, there is
no map—no legend, no ancient street names
or arrows to follow, no red dot assuring me:
you are here—and no place else. If I don't know
where I am, then I am only these heartbeats,
my breaths, the mountains rising and falling
like a wave scrolling across the train's window.
I am alone with the moon on its path, staring
like a blank page, shear and white as the snow
on the peaks echoing back its light. I am this
solitude, never more beautiful, the arc of space
I travel through for a few hours, touching
nothing and keeping nothing, with nothing
to deny the night, the dark pines pointing
to the stars, this life, always moving and still.

Torsos at the Louvre

after Rilke

These are your clavicles balancing what's left
of your shoulders, jutting into the ghostly air
like the persistent nubs of broken-off wings.

This is the face of your chest facing the world,
seeing and speaking for you now, in a language
of forms that have nothing to do with words.

This is your back: accurate, precise, and loyal,
refusing to let its posture go, holding you up
in place, as if you were still completely whole.

These marble veins are your veins flowing
from a heart of stone, the last part that will
crumble, once every part of you has failed

you, unarmed warrior, blind hunter, or lover
without hands or lips—this is you, after you
and all you were meant to be, life beyond

a face, name, or history—no longer struggling
to change what we cannot change, almost free
of the greed of the mind and deeds of the body.

After Barcelona, In Barcelona

After hearing nothing through seven centuries
rising from candles into sooty eyes of *santos*
fixed in the weeping stone of cathedral walls,
after my obsession over the wrinkled hands
of gray couples walking in ascots and pearls
up *Passeig Gracia* every night into oblivion,
after taking down three days of notes, I take
el metro down to *La Arena* on *la Gran Via*,
don't ask if it's gay or straight at the door,
just pay my Euros, get stamped, don't care
if it's techno or trance, or that it's teen night
and I'm thirty-four. I bracket my elbows back
on the bar, not dancing, just watching, thinking
if there's a poem in this city, it's not hanging
in the galleries of Miró's colors, but right here
in the ecstasy of these *kids* dancing in the rain
of red, green, and blue lights over their tattoos.
Not in the rows of Picasso portraits, but here:
these post-modern faces with pierced eyebrows
and bodies grooving in three dimensions at once,
their egos hanging at the end of their cigarettes,
their bell-bottoms dragging the floor in defiance
of their youth that will outlive me, and this city
that will outlive us both. After turning every alley
into a sentence, after hunting through the market
for a kilo of similes, after stirring metaphors over
espressos, waiting for the city to *speak*, tonight
I stand in a poem that isn't mine, but theirs.

Directions to The Beach of the Dead

Go to Europe, go to Spain, in Barcelona, walk
under centuries hanging from the iron lamps
of the Gothic Quarter. Touch the mossy walls
down a Venetian-width street until you reach
La Rambla, move with the drove to the *Mercat,*
but don't touch the plums stacked in pyramids
nor the apples layered like red bricks, don't stare
at the eyes of lamb heads on ice. Buy a cheap map
vanish into *Plaça Catalunya* and study the anatomy
of the subway lines flowing under the city's skin.
Take the red one to *Sants,* count out three Euros
in your palm, buy a RENFE ticket south and wait.
Get on. Ride past the fringe of factories, past
the dusky windows, the laundry on the balconies
of the Catalans who make and serve the *chorizos,*
paellas, and *pimientos*—all the *tapas* you've tasted.

In km-per-hour, listen to piped-in Ravel and Bach
above the clack of tracks through tunnels of rock.
You'll emerge riding the edge of cliffs cantilevered
over the Mediterranean. Pull out your map, follow
the towns' names lettered straight out into the sea
like their piers in Catalán: *Castelldefels, Gavá, Prat de
Llobregat* where Dalí pictured a Madonna protecting
the port, blessing the trade of goods, watching evil.
Minutes before Sitges, recite Lorca who lived there:
verde que te quiero verde / verde que te quiero verde /verde…
though it's not very green at all, you'll ask yourself:
Should I live here? Could I live here? Don't answer—
just get off at Sitges, trickle south from the station
through the capillary of boutique streets, tempting

you with nothing you need. Go on: buy perfumes,
silks, silver rings, sandals you'll wear to walk up
to the city's *catedral* like a fort against the beach.
Wait for the bells and gulls, light a candle, then go—
follow the promenade, past El Hotel Terramar,
past empty stone benches like old men facing
the sea, thinking of places they may never see.

After the promenade, listen for the steel rails
vibrating like a tuning fork still humming from
the pass of the last train. Walk on the tracks until
you reach a small mountain. Smell the names
of flowers you've never known, take pictures
against the wind as you climb up, then down into
a crescent-shaped cove. Take your sandals off,
knead your soles over moon-white stones until
you can't walk anymore, take off your clothes,
lie down between the sun and earth, fall asleep—
past Sitges and Barcelona, past Europe, yourself.
Let the breeze wake you, feel the waves push, pull
at your feet, then take a stone, weigh it in your hand,
bring it to your lips—throw it in, throw another and
another, try to fill the sea with stones and you will
understand why *la Platjes del Mort, la Playa del Muerto*,
the beach where you stand, is named after the dead.

Winter of the Volcanoes: Guatemala

Because rain clouds shade the valley all summer,
they call this their winter, and I'm here, witness
to the rains of August, surrounded by volcanoes.
Volcanoes everywhere, like cathedrals at the end
of every stretch of cobblestone I wobble through.
Volcanoes, triangulating the view in every window,
reading over my shoulders on the terrace at night,
funneling stars between their peaks, threatening
to grumble and leave *la Antigua* to rise a third time
out of ruin. Volcanoes, keeping watch like a council
of four unforgiving gods: Acatenango, Fuego, Agua,
and Pacaya—the one I climbed, step by step through
rows of corn groomed like manes by Mayan hands,
through the quilt work of terrace farmers' patches,
through clouds veiling through pinewood forests,
until I walked in pumice fields, barren as the moon,
if the moon were black, spelled out my name with
freshly minted stones I laid down to claim *I was here*
on this newly kilned rock that in a few eons will be
the soil of the valley, the earth I savor in my coffee,
the dust settling over window sills and counter tops.
I scaled the peak, reached the crater's lip, stood silent
over the cauldron of molten, blood-orange petals,
the pearlescent fire, an open wound weeping smoke,
terrified I might fall, terrified that, for a moment,
I'd let myself be seduced by the pure, living heart
of the raw earth, saying: *here, let me take you back.*

Bargaining with a Goddess
(at the Chichi Market, Guatemala)

after Rigoberta Menchú

The diversity of materials, techniques, and designs of these Guatemalan products
enables the nation's artisans to satisfy the most discerning tastes.
Visite Guatemala 2001

Jade rosaries and letter openers, little jaguars on key rings, paperback
copies of the ancient *Popol Vuh,* shelves lined with plastic temples,
wooden saints, rows of black Christs with hand-painted eyes looking
toward heaven, and a woman the color of a dry rose, fanning her
skirt, showing me a frenzy of hummingbirds and mountain flowers
embroidered in colors truer than my life. *Algo para your wife?* she asks,
leading me to her table where she riffles through her pile of skirts like a
flipbook of flora and fauna. But I'm not married. *O, then algo for your casa*
she orders, shuffling through her placemats, stacking them like tortillas,
insisting I examine the threads of her exquisite stitching—*Mira, mira—*
only 20 Quetzales for you. I pay what she asks, knowing there is more to
her, more than I can know or bargain for: silver bangles and crucifixes,
wooden saints staring into the air, streams of *copal* incense drifting into
faces, bags of fresh rose petals laid out like candy, and hollow piñatas
swaying in the shadows of the market. But how much for the reds,
greens, and yellows of her valley, for her ancient rows of corn, for her
Christian sins, her bleeding knees and *promesas?* How much for her
gods that commanded her flesh out of corn, for her thoughts in *Quiché,*
her forgotten astronomy and eons of history? How much for her cloud
forests, her rain, for her ruins and her village, for her candlelit home and
raw wool blankets? How much for the magic of her needles blossoming
flowers somewhere inside the folds of these mountains no one can own,
under a breadth of priceless stars even my imagination cannot buy.

Pirenópolis, Brazil: Under Protest

The landscape is appalling—palm trees everywhere,
growing as they please, their parallel trunks hatching
the horizon like ruined pillars holding nothing up.
The unkept path leading to my bungalow, taken over
by messy tufts of iris, and the bougainvillea drooping
over everything, blocking the last bit of every sunset
with their sloppy run of fuchsia petals from the roof.

They never close their windows here. I have to listen
to the scuff of their samba feet, Portuguese laughter
fluttering all night through their tacky lace curtains,
their vintage homes held together by raging vines,
each painted a ridiculous pastel color that clashes
with the sound green of the surrounding mountains.

Why, this could hardly be called a village, horses
running through the streets, fireflies swarming about
wild gardenia bushes, a river full of unruly children,
their bright rags tossed on the banks, jumping off
the rickety bridge, its wooden bones about ready
to break, and I'd spend the rest of my life here.

Return from El Cerrado

for V.C.L.

Two days ago, I was below the equator and you
were driving, holding the wheel with one hand, and
my hand with the other. It was summer on the road,
iron-red dust lifting like a ghost, and I was hoping
this: that I belonged wherever I was going with you,
north into the Amazon or south toward São Paulo—
I couldn't tell, it was all green to me, it was all acres
of sky-filled lakes, all waterfalls and streams tearing
through the mountains, it was all mountains, it was
about you and me, the possibility, the odds of
disappearing into you, and your country, into one
of its villages with gables and bell towers peeking
through the landscape. I'd get used to the blooms
bursting through October, frost glazing over July,
you'd teach me Portuguese, I'd teach you Spanish:
mão is *mano, pan* is *pão, amanhã* is *mañana,* but today
I'm at the old grains of my desk again with nothing
changed: the same bouquet of pen-n-pencil stems,
the furniture unmoved, the same color on the walls,
the same books on sagging shelves, and winter here,
a season away from you, a continent against me.

Se pregunta el viajero si sostuvo

el tiempo, andando contra la distancia,

y vuelve adonde comenzó a llorar:

vuelve a gastar su dosis de yo mismo

vuelve a irse con todos sus adioses.

PABLO NERUDA, *Adioses*

The traveler asks himself: if he lived out

a lifetime, pushing the distance away,

does he come back to the place where his grieving began:

squander his dose of identity again,

say his goodbyes again, and go?

trans. BEN BELITT

Silent Family Clips

The projector whirls like a tiny, black time-machine
on the coffee table, a cone of light shoots the dark,
opens a hole in the living room wall like a portal
into lives I never knew, years I don't remember living.
1970 is about ten-seconds long featuring a version
of my brother I never loved, content with hitting
a ball against the graffiti on a city wall, twenty years
before we'd learn to be brothers I the wall breaks
to Miami Beach waves dissolving at my *abuela's* feet,
sauntering down the shore with beauty pageant steps,
her bathing cap flowers fresh as the Art Deco facades
shimmering behind her I fading away to my *abuelo*
standing on the boardwalk at orthodox attention,
his hair once as black as the black of his oxfords,
the circles from his *tabaco* like tree rings dating him
and filling the frame with smoke I the smoke clears
to a mist floating above Niagara Falls, the deluge
a backdrop to a woman who must be my mother,
donning a magenta blouse scribbled with paisleys,
a string of plastic teal beads like a candy necklace
competing against the golden mums and the clock
in a knot garden where she's never been a widow
standing next to *papá* I he speaks into the camera,
but the film is silent, cloud shadows darken over
his dark lips, a voice I can't hear forever I forever
there is a room strung with banners and balloons,
a birthday cake circled by faces like stained glass
lit by dim candle light, faces not yet loved or lost
by a boy who is me I I watch myself close my eyes,
take a breath, make a wish I will never remember.

Papá's Bridge

Morning, driving west again, away from the sun
rising in the slit of the rearview mirror, as I climb
on slabs of concrete and steel bent into a bridge
arcing with all its parabolic y-squared splendor.
I rise to meet the shimmering faces of buildings
above tree tops meshed into a calico of greens,
forgetting the river below runs, insists on running
and scouring the earth, moving it grain by grain.

And for a few inclined seconds every morning
I am twelve years old with my father standing
at the tenth floor window of his hospital room,
gazing at this same bridge like a mammoth bone
aching with the gravity of its own dense weight.
The glass dosed by a tepid light reviving the city
as I watched and read his sleeping, wondering
if he could even dream in such dreamless white:

Was he falling? Was he flying? Who was he, who
was I underneath his eyes, flitting like the birds
across the rooftops and early stars wasting away,
the rush-hour cars pushing through the avenues
like the tiny blood cells through his vein, the I.V.
spiraling down like a string of clear licorice feeding
his forearm, bruised pearl and lavender, colors
of the morning haze and the pills on his tongue.

The stitches healed, while the room kept sterile
with the usual silence between us. For three days
I served him water or juice in wilting paper cups,
flipped through muted soap operas and game shows,
filled out the menu cards stamped Bland Diet.

For three nights I wedged flat strange pillows
around his bed, his body shaped like a fallen S
and mortared in place by layers of stiff percale.

When he was ordered to walk, I took his hand,
together we stepped to the window and he spoke
—*You'll know how to build bridges like that someday*—
today, I cross this city, this bridge, still spanning
the silent distance between us with the memory
of a father and son holding hands, secretly in love.

What's Love Got to Do?

All summer *papá* holds a cigarette out the window of his laser-green Buick, points his lips left to blow the smoke into the mirage of exhaust between rush hour cars. All summer he listens to *La Cubanisima* on AM radio exploding with accounts of how Castro took everything *we* had, how *we'd* get it back someday. All summer he wears polyester ties and his over-polished loafers. All summer I float my arm like a wing out the window as we glide down Coral Way, past storefronts and memories: the 7–11 stops for *Blow-Pops* and *Slurpees*, the square pizzas at Frankie's, the birthday dinners at Canton Rose. All summer I want to ask if he remembers what I remember, but I don't, so he just drives, all summer, keeping a safe distance in the right lane, from our Miami suburb to my uncle's *bodega*, where all summer I price and rotate, mop and bag and save for my own car. All summer I don't want to be me. I don't want to be my father either, eleven years in his windowless office adding and subtracting, wishing and forgetting he could be more. All summer he picks me up at 6:00 and we drive back on the same road, the same mix of cigarettes and Piña Colada air-freshener, the same visors eclipsing our faces, the same silence. All summer I wait for him to say something— anything, like: *I hate grapefruit juice*, or *I can't stand the Navarro's*, or *I've cheated on your mother*, or *I hate this life*. What he did say was: *I love Tina Turner*, every time I took control of the radio and tuned-in to her FM hits. All summer he sang along in his thick Cuban accent (*waus love gotta do/ gotta do wis it*) and whistle through the words he didn't know. Then he'd say something about *Mamá* and him in the 60's dancing to Ike and Tina in Cuba, and pick up the refrain again (*waus love but a secon' hand emoshun*). He embarrassed me with his singing all summer, that summer before his throat swelled, before the weekly visits to Dr. Morad, before the Mitomycin and Hail Marys failed, before he'd never sing again. That summer, when all I managed to mutter was: *Yeah, I love Tina too.*

Revisiting Metaphors at South Point

Light has begun to taper toward the sun, the day
drawn out of the sky, hooded over the pier's planks
reaching into the horizon like a wooden keyboard
veneered with fish scales glinting like silver leaf.
I stand like the piles, tending my shadow which is
twice as long as it was twenty-five years ago when
I stood here, without metaphors for these images,
when light was light, and your face was only itself—
a wordless profile beside me, but enough for a son:
to have his father's hand curled around his finger,
to creak down the pier together, not looking for
philosophy in the eyes of fishermen gutting fish,
nor trying to read the smears of blood like graffiti.
Enough to be just a boy on a Saturday, belonging
to my father, to reach the end of the pier, meet
the simple thrill of wanting to jump in the water,
before it became the sea talking back in similes,
before silence became a figure of speech for you.
Enough to brave the jetty with you holding me
as I leaned over jagged rocks, watching jellyfish
fade in-and-out of the water's lens, years before
I would compare their weak and deliberate pulses
to your last breaths, their vanishing to your death.

Translation for Mamá

What I've written for you, I have always written
in English, my language of silent vowel endings
never translated into your language of silent h's.
> *Lo que he escrito para ti, siempre lo he escrito*
> *en inglés, en mi lengua llena de vocales mudas*
> *nunca traducidas a tu idioma de haches mudas.*

I've transcribed all your old letters into poems
that reconcile your exile from Cuba, but always
in English. I've given you back the *guajiro* roads
you left behind, stretched them into sentences
punctuated with palms, but only in English.
> *He transcrito todas tus cartas viejas en poemas*
> *que reconcilian tu exilio de Cuba, pero siempre*
> *en inglés. Te he devuelto los caminos guajiros*
> *que dejastes atrás, tranformados en oraciones*
> *puntuadas por palmas, pero solamente en inglés.*

I have recreated the *pueblecito* you had to forget,
forced your green mountains up again, grown
valleys of sugarcane, stars for you in English.
> *He reconstruido el pueblecito que tuvistes que olvidar,*
> *he levantado de nuevo tus montañas verdes, cultivado*
> *la caña, las estrellas de tus valles, para ti, en inglés.*

In English I have told you how I love you cutting
gladiolas, crushing *ajo*, setting cups of *dulce de leche*
on the counter to cool, or hanging up the laundry
at night under our suburban moon. In English,
> *En inglés te he dicho cómo te amo cuando cortas*
> *gladiolas, machacas ajo, enfrías tacitas de dulce de leche*
> *encima del mostrador, o cuando tiendes la ropa*
> *de noche bajo nuestra luna en suburbia. En inglés*

I have imagined you surviving by transforming
yards of taffeta into dresses you never wear,
keeping *Papá's* photo hinged in your mirror,
and leaving the porch light on, all night long.

> *he imaginado como sobrevives transformando*
> *yardas de tafetán en vestidos que nunca estrenas,*
> *la foto de papá que guardas en el espejo de tu cómoda,*
> *la luz del portal que dejas encendida, toda la noche.*
> *Te he captado en inglés en la mesa de la cocina*
> *esperando que cuele el café, que hierva la leche*
> *y que tu vida se acostumbre a tu vida. En inglés*
> *has aprendido a adorar tus pérdidas igual que yo.*

I have captured you in English at the kitchen table
waiting for the *café* to brew, the milk to froth,
and your life to adjust to your life. In English
you've learned to adore your losses the way I do.

Abuela's Voices: A Chronicle

i: *I'd rather have a granddaughter who's a whore
than a grandson who's a faggot like you.*

In the empty parking lot of St. Jude's Church
in Westchester, on a summer day, she lets go
and falls to the gritty pavement while I pedal
and pedal and glide without training wheels
for the first time. At last, in perfect balance,
I'm the perfect *hombrecito* she wants me to be,
which I guess means needing nobody's help,
being in control and going wherever I want.
I want to look back at the clapping I hear, see
her standing 4-foot-10, never prouder of me.
On the way back, I'm a knight riding my bike
beside her, the blood drying over her knees
reminds me of the scratches on her forearms
from the guinea hens she strangles every year
for *Nochebuena* in the backyard. But tonight
she sautés chicken for *fricasé*, extra drumsticks
just for me. *Mañana,* she says, while dribbling
sauce over my rice, *tomorrow we'll try the skates.*

ii: *¡Arriba! The ripe ones are all the way at the top.
I need at least ten more—why can't you reach them!*

The leaves filter out her hollers into whispers
at the top of Ms. Pike's mango tree where I am
perched above all the neighborhood's rows
of rooftops, fence lines, and telephone poles.
I'm almost a little god, my body suspended
from my left arm hooked around the trunk,
and my right armed with a broom, hunting
through branches for ripe-colored mangos:

one-third emerald, a third ruby, a third gold
falling from the sky down to *abuela* below me,
scuttling like a hen after every rolling mango
that lands unscathed. Hours later we return
with full buckets swinging on my handlebars.

All afternoon she'll lean over the kitchen sink
skinning mangos, whistling boleros off-key,
pausing every few minutes to remember love.
All afternoon she'll force pound after pound
of sugar into *her mangos,* making her famous
mermelada for her sisters and sisters' friends,
to show off her sweet-thumb and how high
I climbed, how strong her *machito* is getting.

iii: *Soap, batteries, watches—I even sold bloomers
door-to-door en Nueva Yor. I worked like a perra,
pero mira, look, I saved enough to buy our house.*

So the legendary story goes every afternoon
she'd spend stationed at the head of the table,
her stout legs swinging just short of the floor,
while dishing her medley of gossip and sermon
over the telephone to her sisters and neighbors,
interrupting herself to moisten her fingertips
with saliva and thumb through lotto tickets.

Or the tale of how in Cuba she was accused
by *los comunistas* of conspiracy with *la CIA,*
(which I thought was *Sears* mispronounced)
because everyone was envious of her house,
the first one in *Hormiguero* tiled with *mosaico.*
Decades later, I visit the old house, step over
the tiles, moldy and broken. She hadn't lied.

iv: *¿Qué? Those sort of things are not for boys?*

Every day after lunch Mrs. McNulty reads
from *The Lion, the Witch, and the Wardrobe*
while the class keeps their hands busy with
color-by-number, crochet, popsicle-sticks,
or latch-hook rugs like the kit *abuela* made
my father and me return to K-mart because
I'm not a girl, because I'd never be an *artista*.
I sit every afternoon shy at my desk, hating
my empty hands, wanting to disappear into
a magical world behind the wardrobe where
I'd be the noble lion, and *abuela* the witch.

v: *You'll never be anything unless you're rich.*
Put twenty-five cents in your waquita everyday,
and see how much money you'll have in a year.

She empties a half-empty can of *Café Pilón*,
peels apart a brown paper bag and wraps
the can with it. I print my full name, draw
dollar signs and stars with a black marker,
then glue the lid on and cut a slit on top
large enough for quarters and folded bills.
I follow her through the house snooping
underneath everyone's beds and closets
until she decides the best hiding place
for my *waquita* is her underwear drawer.
I can't tell anyone, not even my mother,
she warns, and drops the first quarter in.

vi: *I'll give you and Tania $1000 if you get engaged*
this year—$3000 for the honeymoon, and $2000
for every grandchild you two give me—but no more
than $10,000. She's worth it—a strong woman,
knows how to handle you—and pretty too.

vii: *Abuelo used to write me beautiful poemas like yours*
when we were in love—you got it from him, I bet.

Reaching to just above my elbow, I hold her
by her elbow, steer her through the labyrinth
of supermarket aisles. She looks up to me
from her steps over the beige linoleum tiles,
her eyes occluded sapphires, like a newborn
she repeats herself: *I need frijoles/frijoles negros;*
repeats how I once loved her and *what/what*
happened? I mumble *nothing/nada*, rehearsing
the talk where she is supposed to apologize
and I accept she didn't know any better. But
it's not the right time. All she needs today is
a loaf of *pan/pan, leche/leche*, some *amor/amor.*

viii: *I never want to be hooked up like those viejos*
who can't even eat or even shit by themselves.
¡Ay no! And all those crazy machines tracking
my this or my that with those bleeps and dials,
that electric thing scribbling out my heartbeats
and everyone crowded around me crying like fools,
feeling sorry, not knowing what to do with me.

¡Qué va! My hands tied by the wrists to the bed?
My fingers motioning like scissors to cut me off?

And all those tubes down my throat drowning me
with air so that I can't even speak? I want to go
quickly—but not quietly—I want to go talking
as I have talked all my life. Do you hear me?
Listen, I want to die living—not like this.

Returning Shine

Every other Thursday night I'd snatch
the family's shoes from the eerie bottom
of the closets, carry them away hooked
on my fingers like a proud catch of fish,
spilled on the cold Florida room terrazzo
where my *abuelo* sat barefoot, legs crossed,
whistling as he inspected my offerings,
sorting out the pile by gender and color:
pumps with pumps, oxfords with oxfords
black with black and brown with brown.
After the last pair, I'd take my place
next to him and wait for instructions:

First, a light brush to take off the dust,
followed by a wash with his *special* cloth,
then set aside again in neat rows ready
for a second inspection, his eyes approving
pairs dry enough for polish to be applied
only with my middle and index fingertips,
with quick, light taps—*así, así, suavecito*—
he'd say, holding my hand by the wrist,
guiding it over the leather, teaching me
how to firm the shoe over my fist, palm
the brush, and flick my wrist in rhythm.

And even after I'd learned to do it *right*,
even after I learned I would outlive him,
I pretended not to, knowing somehow,
someday I would need to recall our ritual
and him playing his best horse hair brush

like a violin bow across the shoe's vamp,
turning his wisps and strokes into music.
That after years of becoming—of saying,
doing, and going—I'd need to return to
the simple pleasure of returning a shine.

Only Brothers

We carved an entire range of mountains
out of styrofoam blocks, covered their peaks
with sand for snow, the slopes with pines,
the valleys with fall maples and live oaks.
We made great rivers flow on the illusion
of tin foil crinkled and painted royal blue,
crossed them with mighty balsa bridges.
We placed townspeople where we wanted:
gazing into the shops, gathered at the chapel,
or waiting for the train, lapping obediently
under our command around the village
that took us six years to build, and one day,
in the backyard, we set it on fire, quietly
stood by the flames and let it all vanish.

Then Someday

for Bombón y Choco

Ooh we were cool—weren't we—low-cut-button-fly-black-silk cool. Cool
as our unbuttoned shirts, Italian chinos, and designer underwear. Cool-
er than the doorman at *Swirl,* walking past him with our *look but don't
touch* look, like everyone should know us. Damn we were gorgeous—
weren't we—combed-eyebrows-and-dark-rum-skin gorgeous, in sling-
back heels and square-toe loafers, stepping to the beat all the way to the
end of the bar. Yeah, we were fierce, dangerous—weren't we—too good
for everyone except the bartenders who lit our cigarettes and knew
how we liked our martinis: dirty, straight-up, twist; and our pours
of Dambuie glinting over ice, water on the side. Every night was our
night—wasn't it—we made it happen on the dance floor, going down
low on the grind, shaking our booties years before Beyoncé. We were
hot—weren't we—hotter than the ruby lasers piercing the clouds of
smoke around us. But it was never enough—was it—even at 4am,
cruising the causeway with the top down, the dark palms like sleep-
ing angels, the reflection of skyscrapers wavering over the bay like a
sunken city, and the safranin glow of street lights diffused above the
mainland sky. God, it was beautiful—wasn't it—driving home with
the perfect song on the radio and the three of us singing out loud to
the stars as if we had a hundred years to live. And we did—didn't
we? Someday we'd cover our walls with photos, look into our eyes
and not recognize the world we once held in them: all the parties
with our glasses raised to the camera, all the birthday dinners hud-
dled around the table, all the sunsets at the beach feeding seagulls.
Someday Kenita, Jorge, Raymond, and my father would die, and
we'd learn to brave those seconds in the mirror before our faces be-
come our faces. Someday we'd be almost everything we wanted to
be and find ourselves: the Puerto Rican boy still hearing the call of

coquís, the Nuyorican girl still swinging to the rhythm of *el barrio,* and the Cuban *guajiro* still imagining fields of sugarcane jutting into the sky—together again, driving back home through the city in which we learned to love each other, listening to our voices come back to us from the night.

The Perfect City Code

for M.C.

1(a) Streets shall be designed *Euro-Style* with 300-ft right-of-ways, benches, and flowered traffic circles, to provide a distinct sense of beauty, regardless of cost.

1(b) There shall be a canopy of trees; these shall be your favorite: *Giant Royal Palms,* 25-ft high, whereas their fronds shall meet in cathedral-like arches with a continuous breeze that shall slip in our sleeves and flutter against our bodies so as to produce angel-like sensations of eternity.

1(c) There shall be bushes; these shall also be your favorite: *Tea Roses* @2-ft o.c. to provide enough blooms for casual picking; whereas said blooms shall spy on us from crystal glasses set next to the stove, over coffee-table books, or in front of mirrors.

2(a) Sidewalks shall be crack-proof and 15-ft wide for continuous, side-by-side conversations; painted either a) *Sunflower-Brown,* b) *Mango Blush,* or c) *Rosemont Henna*; whereas such colors shall evoke, respectively: the color of your eyelashes, of your palms, the shadows on your skin.

3(a) There shall be an average of one (1) Parisian-style café per city block, where I shall meet your eyes, dark as espresso, above the rim of your demitasse, and hold your hand like a music box underneath the table; where we shall exercise all those romantic, cliché gestures we were always too smart for.

3(b) There shall also be one (1) open-air market per city block to facilitate the purchase of tulips, raspberries, white chocolate baci, and other gourmet items to lavish our lives; whereas every night I shall watch you through a glass of brandy as you dice fresh cilantro and dill, disappearing into the scent steaming around you.

4(a) Utility poles or structures that obstruct our view shall not be permitted. At all times we shall have one of the following vistas: birds messaging across the sky, a profile of mountains asleep on their backs, or a needle-point of stars.

5(a) There shall be an *Arts District* and we shall float through gallery rooms on Saturday afternoons perplexed by the pain or conflict we can't feel in a line or a splatter of color; works that glorify or romanticize tragedy shall not be allowed.

5(b) There shall also be a *Historic District* to provide residents with a distinct sense of another time. We shall live there, in a loft with oak floors, a rose-marble mantle where our photos will gather; our years together will compete with the age of the brick walls and cobble stones below our vine-threaded balcony.

(*) Without exception, there shall be a central square with a water fountain where we shall sit every evening by the pageantry of cherubs; where we shall listen to the trickle of their coral mouths; where I shall trust the unspoken; where you shall never again tell me there's nothing here for you, nothing to keep you, nothing to change your mind.

Empty Crosswords

for C.S.B.

For fifteen days in my apartment, I watch you
obsessed with your puzzles, mumbling words

   twelve across: conflicted or diverted from attention...

at the dining table, the low lamplight haloed above
you, your pen casting shadows against the grain,
filling in rows and columns with the will of a poet

   fourteen down: standing apart; marked by an absence...

every night on the chaise writing against your lap,
lifting your eyes to scan the courtyard and pluck
letters from the dead bushes in the moonlight

six across: a gem set alone or a card game played alone...

on my bed, your torso bearing down on the points
of your elbows eventually buckling into a sleeping
still-life: a pair of defaced reading glasses resting
on a dictionary parted open to a field of *m* words,
a tabled glass of flat seltzer, the cat perpendicular
to your feet, and my face parallel to your back

   three down: a heartfelt desire for something out of reach...

you don't read *my* clues prompting you to stay,
to fall in love, if not with me, with my Spanish,
with Miami's palm cafés and neon-paved streets,
its *caribe-blue* twilight and *café-con-leche* mornings

nineteen across: a prospective or expected condition...

you could bartend for a while, save tips for a car,
I'd get a bigger place for us, right on the beach

one across: to retire, give up, or abandon; to surrender...

you pack your things: toothbrush, incense, tapes,
and your crosswords, but leave me with a puzzle,
all the blank spaces you'll never fill with words:

two down: to pass out of sight; to pass out of existence . . .

What Is Not Mine

for B.L.

I wake to find you've left, and left a note: *Please*
wait for me, I'll be right back scribbled over the seal
of an envelope with your key, just in case I want
to leave your home that I've borrowed two days.
I don't know where anything is or belongs, only
that it is exactly January in the windows, as I wait,
a thing among the stillness of things that are not
mine: the upside-down cups I haven't drunk from,
stacks of plates like faces I've never met, the ferns
I've never watered, books in rows like an audience
that has watched us undress, the sheets iced over
your bed, a bud vase on your nightstand, next to
the black hands of a clock like a mime gesturing
an end to our time together. I'll leave, leaving only
the swipe of my hand over the bathroom mirror,
whiskers on a razor, a mug of thickened coffee,
traces of my cologne and cigarettes on a pillow.
And my only defense will be that I must return
to what's mine, not wanting to, but having to
become who I was, before I was here, unsure
of just how the bare branches can bear winter.

Sending Palms in a Letter

for N.M.

I received your letter today—thanks—along with
the crayon sketches of yourself in the corn fields,
there, where you are. I think I understand now,
from what you wrote and how you drew yourself—
with a giant frown and your hands in the air full
of refusal—what it must feel like for you, stranded
without bearings, towered by those terrible stalks,
feeling the empty weight of that awful mid-west
sky above rows of green husk and golden spears.
And you, panicking, looking for a way out, back
here to yourself, to the palm trees that you miss.
I tried sketching a few of them, hoping to send
their fronds fluttering like a line of ballerina arms
brushing at my window and bowing to the wind,
even tried to draw the sea for you: waves erasing
footprints and the tufts of wild grasses keeping
the mellow dunes from gusting away. If you leave
don't come back, keep going, though I'm not sure
any place can complete us or completely ruin us.
Some days I feel I've loved the palms and sea
long enough and want to leave myself, but where?
To keep watching corn grow or the palms sway—
our question may not be a matter of where, but
of how long we have to do all we want to, now
that we're older, certain of this one life, uncertain
of the words we need for even the simplest things
——————————how I miss you, for instance.

Three Unendings

for C.A.B.

I | Not this Poem

I'll open with the sunset, a field of wild grasses waving
back and forth in the acute light, changing from brown
to bands of gold along the causeway. Then recapture
the slim shadows of palm trees striping the pavement,
perhaps explore a few metaphors: mangroves clinging
at the fringes, the islands orphaned without bridges.
I'll transition the seventh line into that night at the end
of the dock, our taut fish lines pulling at the silent sea,
which will yield nothing to us. Thus, I'll turn the poem
into an epiphany having something to do with the stars
that I'll fade into a morning walk, our sandals crushing
bits of shell, which I'll describe as *calcified* and *forgotten*,
then close without ever mentioning you, how I knew
from our courteous gestures in the room, that our first
weekend in Key Largo would be our last and the last
line or two of a poem I'd have to finish someday.

II | Last Lines

I pull out your copy of Neruda's poems left
on my shelf. I read *"Tus Manos"* inspiring me to write
another poem about your hands holding a cigarette,
gesturing with our old conversations about Botticelli
or the cosmos over goblets of red wine on the beach
with seashells and stones we'd collect and place along
the window sills as if they'd grow soft with moonlight.
I read *"Tu Risa"* wanting to trace your laughter back
to when I hadn't written about the days we'd walk
together on the boardwalk as if the sea didn't matter,
paying no attention to the senate of stars governing us.
Then I turn to a poem you book-marked with a petal,
flat as the page it kept, turning brown at the edges,
but its heart still scarlet and velvet with want, pressed
between titles: *"El Olvido/Oblivion"* and *"Siempre/Always."*

III | Elegant Endings

A foggy night, a long silver train, someone's hand
pressed on the glass, crystallized breaths eclipsing
a face in a window, slowly moving past someone
left with smoke clinging at their feet—that ending.
Or the one with the glass shells of runway lights—
cobalt, carmine, and jade dotting a stretch of tarmac
below a plane lifting someone into the hull of night.
Or maybe, the grand good-bye kiss in Paris black
and white at the beginning or end of some war—
another great ending—elegant, noble, final. But
this is not a movie. I'm still driving without a script
around your house, spying through the windshield
into the tempera light of your bedroom window,
insisting that you are there, just as I remember you:
reading Cisneros' poems under your halogen lamp,
feeling as alone as Cuba, or playing Mercedes Sosa.
Are you on the balcony finishing another portrait,
or another canvas of perfect palm trees? Are you
sleeping, dreaming of what while the earth spins
and I drive around you again, around the silences
we've slammed behind doors, or never answered,
around apologies I brought with roses and notes,
remembering everything—the scent of wet coral
across your shoulders, the rise of your breath filling
your lean torso, the specks of paint on your hands—
as I circle below your window once more, trying
to catch that one last glimpse of your silhouette
that will let me drive away, vanish beyond the lights
at the end of your street—for good—that ending.

Should we have stayed at home and thought of here?

ELIZABETH BISHOP, *Questions of Travel*

When I was a Little Cuban Boy

O José can you see . . . that's how I sang it, when I was
a *cubanito* in Miami, and *América* was some country
in the glossy pages of my history book, someplace
way north, everyone white, cold, perfect. *This Land
is my Land*, so why didn't I live there, in a brick house
with a fireplace, a chimney with curlicues of smoke.
I wanted to wear breeches and stockings to my *chins*,
those black pilgrim shoes with shinny gold buckles.
I wanted to eat yams with the Indians, shake hands
with *los negros*, and dash through snow I'd never seen
in a one-horse hope-n-say? I wanted to speak in British,
say really smart stuff like *fours core and seven years ago*
or *one country under God, in the visible.* I wanted to see
that land with no palm trees, only the strange sounds
of flowers like petunias, peonies, impatience, waiting
to walk through a door someday, somewhere in God
Bless America and say, *Lucy, I'm home, honey. I'm home.*

Looking for Blackbirds, Hartford

Your postcard from Varadero Beach is on my dresser at home,
where the surf of it rolls day and night making mild Cuban sounds.
WALLACE STEVENS *in a letter to* JOSÉ RODRIGUEZ FEO

8/16
Ladies in charcoal and pink Chanel suits
sip hot Chai from glass mugs at Michael's.
They mind the afternoon with eyes fixed
on the side of their faces, like blackbirds.

10/14
The rose-thatched gazebo at Elizabeth Park
has bared itself into a cloud of thorny vines
where even blackbirds do not perch.

11/1
Along a row of *Perfect-Six* town homes,
a woman matted by a field of red brick
caws out from a third story window like
a blackbird wanting other blackbirds.

12/19
Near the end of fall the black leaves
look like feathers strewn over lawns.

12/21
After the first snowfall nothing remains
black, not even the night. Nothing breaks
the white reverence, not even a blackbird.

1/5
The reservoir has hardened into a bed of ice
expanding, groaning. It's the only sound I hear
complaining of winter through the mountain.

1/28
Airplanes pass, their shadows like blackbirds
landing on the snowy fields before the runway.

2/3
The buildings downtown stand like chess pieces
in a stalemate against the frozen riverfront
that will not break until a blackbird flies.

2/24
The Portuguese men in heavy black coats
gather like blackbirds at *La Estrella* heckling
over Old World days and the World Cup.

3/18
All the bakery cases along Franklin Avenue
in Little Italy, glitter with sprinkled cannoli,
anise candies, and iced cookies. But no pies.

4/2
At the bus stop on Park and Main, I catch
humming birds hovering in the rainforest eyes
of *puertorriqueños.* Where are my *pájaros negros?*

4/13
On the telephone lines dripping with snow
in my window, there ought to be blackbirds,
they ought to be slitting the sky wide open.

A Little Hartford Music

for C.S.

When she plays, she plays all night for no one.
Though tonight, from my window across our street,
I'm listening to her storming up Segovia in the frame
of her window, which she doesn't dream of leaving
because every place is less than paradise, she insists—
Just live where you live. And I'd like to believe her, but
there's dissonance between her strums at midnight
and what she gossips to me about her life over
Welsh cakes and tepid cups of loose Darjeeling tea.

There's no life like hers: a drunk brother calling her
an epileptic bitch, a daily 1200 mg dose of Depakote
making her hands tremble like tissue, but keeping her
mind steady, and a Catholic beauty-pageant mother
showering her with make-up kits and rosaries, which
she prays as much as she plays, because she believes:
when you've been as close to death as I have, honey,
you gotta believe in something besides yourself—

And so, isn't every life *like* hers? I believe that
when she plays alone for no one but herself,
she plays for the same reason I listen—to leave,
cross through the sky on chords and bridges from
her guitar, ride with her notes like milkweed seeds
out of her window, and drift past the attentive rows
of oily street poles and trash cans, all the way down
to the moon perched at the end of Grandview Terrace.
Surely, when she plays Ravel or Bach, it is to be
someplace else, where her body is healed and she
is absolute music—not here, breathing and fractured.

How Can You Love New York?

Do you buy white chrysanthemums and tangelos
at your favorite Korean corner every Thursday,
leave them in an alley you've ignored too long
and say: surprise my little apple pie, I love you?
Or *cab it* to Chinatown on a Saturday morning
and ask the woman with marquise-shaped eyes
behind the *Pearl River* counter adding your bill
in Cantonese, to come spend the night with you?
Do you kiss the Chelsea boys on the lips, grab
their bulging Diesel-Jeans and say God-damn it,
I love this town. Is New York a gorgeous man,
or a stunning woman you take uptown to dinner
and complement the way her long, silky black
avenues fall across her streets. After how many
Brie and San Pellegrino picnics in Central Park,
and shows at the MOMA, do you decide it's love,
but it's just not going to work, without therapy.
How many times will you have to raise your eyes
from garbage, flyers, and gum blotches to the sky
scrapers, and scream, I forgive you NY, NY for
cussing at me and shoving me, for trying to take
over my life, for not listening or calling me back.
How many nights will you spend thinking it over
with the rain sheer as the vodka in your martini,
looking out a bar window at the mélange of lights
floating over the wet pavement with possibilities.
What makes you believe this is it, this is *the* one
you can lose yourself to forever and never want
to leave. How do you know the city isn't lying?

Letter from Nowhere

for D.A.P.

Pour yourself some of that good bourbon of yours in a crystal glass, play *La Traviata* again, sit in your living room, and write me a good, long letter. Tell me again how I'm supposed to tilt my head back, follow the arias with my eyes, let the sound cascade through me. Let me hear you weep again as Violetta dies singing soprano at Alfredo's feet. And after the final act, when all the dead rise and bow to applause and bravos, light one of your Cuban cigars. Remind me of the aroma, describe the exhales of smoke eddying around you and your shelves filled with scrimshaw and fossils. Tell me again how beautiful they are simply for having survived this long. What were the colors of your orchids, the titles of the books I should read, the names of your parents and grandparents crumbling in photos? Tell me their stories, which are your stories now. Let me remember what you remember. Write to me about the South, about Asheville and your cabin where I've never been, tell me about the flagstones you laid, one by one, down the hill to the creek, how you've swum naked, watched the circuit of stars turn the summer nights on, and still refuse to believe a lifetime is enough to go peacefully. Then go to your bedroom, lie under the frayed lamplight in the frame of your great-grandfather's bed, and write something my father would've never told me, tell me you miss me. Include a quote from one of the ancients you've read, tell me again how they live forever, how you want to live forever too. Write and teach me once more, let me hold your words.

Listening at Reading Farm, an Elegy

for T.G.

The weathervane on the roof was turning, the grate of its black iron was grumbling through the attic like a ghost. The farm bell was grazing its shell in the tower, and the wind chimes were gossiping in the vernacular of lavender and heather in your garden. Mary was orchestrating dinner—an operetta of pot clangs, whisking whisks, and chops on the cutting block. Naxcie was pinging through the silverware, and Alyx was tic-toc-ing in the hammock by the pond, gazing up through the pines for a different life. The wind had pushed through the front door into the living room, stirred a cloud of white roses on your credenza, tipped over a photo, riffled through a magazine, and left through the screen door screeching like a violin. Stacy and Mike were nailing hemlock planks for a new footbridge to the red, hollow barn not yet ready for winter and the Belgian horses that would never arrive. Their blows were echoing back from the mountains as far away as Cornish, where Max was imagining Saint-Gaudens sculptures gracing his grounds. A Vermont breeze was joggling the apple tree, apples were striking the table like a slow drum in the terrace, and you were speaking about dusk strumming the birches at Sunapee, about love, about disease and how you may want to, need to, decide to, end your life, the last time I heard you and the weather vane turning, the black iron grumbling, the farm bell grazing its shell.

No More Than This, Provincetown

Today, home is a cottage with morning
in the yawn of an open window. I watch
the crescent moon, like a wind-blown sail,
vanish. Blue slowly fills the sky and light
regains the trust of wildflowers blooming
with fresh spider webs spun stem to stem.
The room rises with the toasting of bread,
a stick of butter puddling in a dish, a knife
at rest, burgundy apples ready to be halved,
a pint of blueberries bleeding on the counter,
and little more than this. A nail in the wall
with a pair of disembodied jeans, a red jersey,
and shoes embossed by the bones of my feet
and years of walking. I sit down to breakfast
over the nicks of a pinewood table and I am,
for a moment, not afraid of being no more
than what I hear and see, no more than this:
the echo of bird songs filling an empty vase,
the shadow of a sparrow moving through
the shadow of a tree, disturbing nothing.

Crossing Boston Harbor

The horn blares—once—twice—sounding like
iron, a dull and heavy slap across the wind's face.

And if the wind could have a face, it would resemble
these strangers, blank as paper dolls propped up

against the railing as the propeller torque vibrates
through the vessel, slowly peeling the hull away

from the barnacled dock, the limp ropes coiled
like dry roses on the metal deck, the anchor up

like a rusty bow hung on the bow, and we move
all together, at the same speed, to the same point.

The ferry's chine makes an incision across the bay,
its churned waters bleed a wake of lustrous blue

behind us as we head west, scanning the coastline
nested with gables and fringed with flocks of sails,

their peaks waning out of sight into memory, until
there's nothing left to measure my distance against.

So much of my life spent like this—suspended,
moving toward unknown places and names or

returning to those I know, corresponding with
the paradox of crossing, being nowhere yet here,

leaning into the wind and light, uncertain of what
I might answer the woman to my right, anchored

in a flutter of cottons and leaning over the stern,
should she lift her eyes from the sea toward me

and ask: *So, where are you from?*

Mexican Almuerzo in New England

for M.G.

Word is praise for Marina, up past 3:00 a.m. the night before her flight,
preparing and packing the *platos tradicionales* she's now heating up in
the oven while the *tortillas* steam like full moons on the stovetop. Dish
by dish she tries to recreate Mexico in her son's New England kitchen,
taste-testing *el mole* from the pot, stirring everything: *el chorizo-con-papas,
el picadillo, el guacamole.* The spirals of her stirs match the spirals in her
eyes, the scented steam coils around her like incense, suffusing the air
with her folklore. She loves Alfredo, as she loves all her sons, as she
loves all things: *seashells, cacti, plumes, artichokes.* Her hand calls us to
circle around the kitchen island, where she demonstrates how to fold
tacos for the *gringo* guests, explaining what is *hot* and what is *not,* trying
to describe tastes with English words she cannot savor. As we eat, she
apologizes: *not as good as at home, pero bueno…* It is the best she can do
in this strange kitchen which Sele has tried to disguise with *papel picado*
banners of colored tissue paper displaying our names in piñata pink,
maíz yellow, and Guadalupe green—strung across the lintels of the patio
filled with talk of an early spring and *do you remembers* that leave an
after-taste even the *flan* and *café negro* don't cleanse. Marina has finished.
She sleeps in the guest room while Alfredo's paintings confess in the
living room, while the papier-mâché skeletons giggle on the shelves,
and shadows lean on the porch with rain about to fall. Tomorrow our
names will come down and Marina will leave with her empty clay pots,
feeling as she feels all things: *velvet, branches, honey, stones.* Feeling what
we all feel: home is a forgotten recipe, a spice we can find nowhere, a
taste we can never reproduce, exactly.

Chilo's Daughters Sing for Me in Cuba

They folded and shaped each banana leaf
like a paper flower with their calloused fingers
to make the *tamales* filled with thirty ears
of cornmeal ground by hand. They helped
Ramon with the slaughter yesterday, seasoned
the pork overnight with salt, cumin, bay leaves.
They culled through every grain of wild rice
and every pound of black beans they could buy
on the black market. They sold three months
of soap rations for a string of garlic, crushed
the garlic, had enough olive oil to make *mojito*
for the *yuca*. They pulled the *yuca* from the soil
of their father's field this afternoon—washed it,
cut it, boiled it—until its heart bloomed open,
tender and white as its flower. They prepared
jugs of watermelon *refresco* and set the table
for twenty with borrowed plates and tin cups—
but no napkins. Now, they serve their dishes,
stand around us, and begin singing a cappella
for me, glad I've come to see them again, to sit
at their table, eat what their hands have made,
listen to their songs. Rosita sings old boleros
for our *tíos* and *tías* still in love with love.
Nivia sings *danzones* to honor our grandfathers
who'll be buried in the same ground they tilled.
Xiomara sings the old *décima* verses of *guajiros*
who made poetry out of cutting sugarcane.
And we all sing *Guantanamera*, over and over
again—*Guantanamera* because today the food
is plentiful, the earth continues to give them
what they need—*Guantanamera* for the lyrics

that praise the good people of this country
where the palms grow—*guajira Guantanamera*
because the revolution that never ends will
never change them, their stories, this land.

Visiting tía Aida

For thirty-five years she's watched Old Havana—
seen chorus-lines of columns strip to naked stone,
and stucco walls shrivel, then blossom with weeds.
She's pitied the churches and palaces aging faster
than her, counted the iron lampposts of *El Prado*
burning out, one by one, along with her memories
of *those* five sisters in Miami, so many years away
from her now. She waits in a second-story *vivienda*
atop a dark flight of stairs she can no longer climb,
slowly falling apart with the rest of *La Habana vieja.*

Rain begins, stiffens the lines of dingy clothes
waving across broken lunettes of stained-glass
like war torn flags. She curses *la revolución*—
why she had to stay, why they have to leave—
the cracked wall behind her, white and wrinkled
as her hand. She reaches for a bottle of violet water
and a jar of ointment on the metal tray-table
with a worn deck of cards and a rotary phone
she insists still works, though nobody calls.
No es fácil—she complains—*It's not easy*—
the black-market prices, the daily blackouts—
No es fácil—her age, this loneliness she has
almost accepted as fate—*No es fácil estar sola.*

Yet everywhere there are precious things
suggesting she has not given up on herself,
on beauty: dusty silk flowers in a wall vase,
poor geisha figurines on her coffee table,
thin velvet pillows, vintage photos pressed
under her dresser's glass top. *Look*, she says,
holding up a pink sateen gown from her niece,

which she's rending to make a new bedspread—
It'll be beautiful, when I'm done—tears dammed
in her eyes, clear as the rain weeping through
the frail balcony hanging above the street
like a petal about to fall from a dying rose.

My Campo Santo

Here I am my father working the sugar mill,
swimming in the valley swales. I am my mother
sweeping the dirt floor of her childhood home,
and selling oranges by the side of a road. Here,
my *abuelo* is the scent of night jasmine, my *abuela*
is the silvery dust settling on a moonlit orchard.
Here I'm the arms of *guajiros* swinging machetes
and pulling up red potatoes. I am their breaths
singing their country songs, praising the land
or cursing it, keeping them alive. Here I've been
a *taíno* spearing fish and husking corn, a slave
drumming stories, a *criollo* counting doubloons
and pieces of eight. I've been a poet rhyming
and dreaming in Spanish, a *yanqui* buying
dictators, a bearded rebel asleep with his rifle.

Here, I watch the wind reborn, my eyes rise
with clouds taking to the sky like new souls.
I hear the rain gossiping, know the secrets
of how the red earth makes green *guayabas_*
out of nothing, and I rest with the lakes
cupped in the hands of the green valleys' hills.
This is where I belong—among the blades
of sugarcane fields waving like wild manes,
the tropical sky sequined with twilight stars,
and banana leaves trembling in the breeze
like butterflies. For a moment or a lifetime
everything is mine, and yet all I can keep
is the bare, silent spaces between mountains,
the pause between the rustle of every palm.

where it begins—where it ends

somewhere somehow
the wind blows and the dust sweeps in
a mountain is pared down through a cracked window
a cliff's chin is shaved underneath the front door
a dune is stolen from a desert and comes to rest on my desk
a parched field is raped over the edge of a frame
ripe stones are ground on blocks of consumed books
weathered into souls over an array of aging photos
and dead things burn alive gingerly settling out of beams
into ghosts of gray ash in the morning light, floating
almost invisible, arriving in the quiet air of my room
from places I've never been until the wind blows again

ACKNOWLEDGEMENTS

Grateful acknowledgement is made to the editors of the following publications in which these poems first appeared, sometimes in earlier versions: *Bellevue Literary Review*: "A Little Hartford Music," and "Listening to Reading Farms, an Elegy"; *Caduceus*: "Elegant Endings," "A Poet in Venice," and "Letter from Nowhere" (as "Letter for Letter"); *Carin*: "When I was a Little Cuban Boy"; *Connecticut Review*: "Papá's Bridge," "Return from El Cerrado," and "Mexican Almuerzo in New England"; *The Cream City Review*: "Perfect City Code"; *Indiana Review*: "Time as Art in The Eternal City," and "We're Not Going to Malta..."; *New England Review*: "Crossing Boston Harbor"; *Notre Dame Review*: "Empty Crosswords" (as "November Crosswords"); *Ploughshares*: "Abuela's Voices: A Chronicle" and "What's Love Got to Do?"; *Puerto del Sol*: "Winter of the Volcanoes: Guatemala"; *32 Poems*: "No More Than This, Provincetown."

"Sending Palms in a Letter," and "Revisiting Metaphors at South Point" appeared in *Tigertail, A South Florida Annual*, Campbell McGrath, ed. (Tigertail Productions, Volume 1, 2003); "Returning Shine" first appeared in *Emergence of Man into the 21st Century*, Patricia L. Munhall, Ed Madden, Virginia M. Fitzsimons, eds. (Jones and Bartlett Publishers, 2002); "Silent Family Clips" (as "35mm Clips") and "Where it begins—where it ends" (as "How it Begins—How it Ends") appeared in *American Diaspora: Poetry of Displacement*, Virgil Suárez and Ryan G. Van Cleave, eds. (University of Iowa Press, 2001); "Papá's Bridge" appeared in *The Idiot's Guide to Writing Poetry*, Nikki Moustaki, ed. (Alpha Books, 2001). "Winter of the Volcanoes: Guatemala," "Looking for Blackbirds, Hartford," and "Return from El Cerrado" appeared in *MisPoesias* (http://www.mispoesias.com); "We're Not Going to Malta..." appeared as the poem of the day for July 24, 2004 in the *Poetry Daily* (http://poems.com); "Last Lines" appeared in *Beltway Literary Quarterly* (http://www.washingtonart.com).

Some of these poems appeared in "Nowhere But Here," a chapbook published by the Hill-Stead Museum (2004) in conjunction with the Sunken Garden Poetry Festival in Farmington, Connecticut. My thanks to artistic director Alison Myers for her many talents and enthusiasm. For support and assistance I am also grateful to the Bread Loaf Writers Conference John Ciardi Fellowship, Central Connecticut State University, the Virginia Center for the Creative Arts Residency Fellowship, the St. Andrews College Ronald D. Bayes Writer-in-Residence Fellowship, and the State of Florida Individual Artist Fellowship.

Aplausos for Nikki Moustaki, Naomi Ayala, Christopher Louvet, Ted Wojtasik, Patti Hartmann, and Stuart Bernstein for their invaluable help with this collection. *Mil gracias* to Terri Horne, Elizabeth Hurst Downs, Mark Moody,

Geneva Stone, Liliana Valenzuela and Michael Zoll for their friendship and help with individual poems. And *un abrazo caribeño* for my spiritual band of *músicos, poetas, y locos*: Sandra Cisneros, Campbell McGrath, Susana Restrepo, Bernard McKenna, Ito Romo, Cheryl Simkins, Meredith Beattie and especially, Mark Neveu, for his endless encouragement, advice, and love.

ABOUT THE AUTHOR

Richard Blanco was made in Cuba, assembled in Spain, and imported to the United States—meaning his mother, seven months pregnant, and the rest of the family arrived as exiles from Cuba to Madrid, where he was born. Only forty-five days later, the family emigrated once more and settled in New York City, then eventually in Miami, where he was raised and educated. Blanco has traveled extensively and has lived in several places, including Guatemala, Brazil, Connecticut, where he was Assistant Professor of Creative Writing and Latino Literature, and Washington D.C., where he taught at Georgetown and American Universities. His acclaimed first book of poetry, *City of a Hundred Fires*, explores the yearnings and negotiation of cultural identity as a Cuban-American and received the Agnes Starrett Poetry Prize from the University of Pittsburgh Press (1998). His poems have appeared in *The Nation, Ploughshares, Indiana Review, Michigan Quarterly Review, TriQuarterly Review, New England Review*, and several anthologies including *The Best American Poetry 2000, Great American Prose Poems, Bread Loaf Anthology of New American Poets*, and *American Poetry: The Next Generation*. He has been featured on National Public Radio's *All Things Considered* and at various conferences and venues around the nation; he is recipient of the John Ciardi Fellowship from the Bread Loaf Writers Conference, a Florida Artist Fellowship, and a Residency Fellowship from the Virginia Center for the Creative Arts. A builder of bridges and poems, Blanco holds both a Bachelor of Science degree in Civil Engineering and a Master in Fine Arts in Creative Writing.